LIVES
AND
TIMES

Martin Luther King Jr.

Peter and Connie Roop

Heinemann Library
Chicago, Illinois

©1998 Reed Educational & Professional Publishing
Published by Heinemann Library,
an imprint of Reed Educational & Professional Publishing,
100 N. LaSalle, Suite 1010
Chicago, IL 60602

Customer Service 888-454-2279

Printed in Hong Kong / China
Designed by Ken Vail Graphic Design, Cambridge
Illustrated by Sean Victory

03 02 01 00
10 9 8 7 6 5 4 3 2

Library of Congress Cataloging-in-Publication Data
Roop, Peter.
    Dr. Martin Luther King Jr./Peter and Connie Roop.
        p. cm. -- (Lives and times)
    Includes bibliographical references and index.
    Summary: An introductory biography of the Baptist minister and
civil rights leader whose philosophy and practice of nonviolent
civil disobedience helped African Americans win many battles for
equal rights.
    ISBN 1-57572-560-6 (lib. bdg.)
    1. King, Martin Luther, 1929 - 1968 -- Juvenile literature. 2. Afro -
Americans -- Biography -- Juvenile literature. 3. Civil rights workers -- United
States -- Biography -- Juvenile literature. 4. Baptists - United States -- Clergy --
Biography -- Juvenile literature. 5. Afro-Americans -- Civil rights -- History--
20th century -- Juvenile literature. 6. Civil rights movements -- United States --
History -- 20th century -- Juvenile literature. (1. King, Martin Luther, Jr. 1929-
1968. 2. Clergy. 3. Civil rights workers. 4. Afro-Americans - Biography.) I.
Roop, Connie II. Title. III. Series: Lives and Times (Crystal Lake, Ill.)
E185.97.K5R59 1997
323'.092 --dc21
    (B)   97-13732
                                                              CIP
                                                               AC

Acknowledgments
The author and publisher are grateful to the following for permission to reproduce copyright photographs:
Accociated Press pp. 18, 21; British Library p. 22;
Corbis-Bettmann / UPI pp. 16, 17, 19, 23; Martin, Phil, p. 20.

Cover photograph: Corbis-Bettmann / UPI
Special thanks to Betty Root for her comments on the preperation of this book.
Every effort has been made to contact copyright holders of any material reproduced in this book. Any omissions will be
rectified in subsequent printings if notice is given to the publisher.

Especially for Erika. Your sense of justice will make the world a better place for everyone.

Some words are shown in bold, **like this**. You can find out what they mean by looking in the glossary. The glossary also
helps you say difficult words.

Contents

Part One

Martin Luther King Jr. was born on January 15, 1929 in Atlanta, Georgia. As a young boy he loved to play football, baseball, and the piano.

When Martin was young, there were **laws** that kept whites and African Americans separate. One law said children like Martin could not go to school with white children.

Martin wanted to change **laws** that treated African Americans unfairly. He studied hard and went to Morehouse College in Atlanta when he was only 15 years old.

Martin wanted to be a **minister**. He went to study at Crozer **Seminary** in Pennsylvania. There he learned about Mohandas Gandhi, the **nonviolent** leader.

Martin met Coretta Scott when he was studying in Boston. In 1953 they were married. Coretta helped Martin with his work throughout his life.

In 1955, Martin received his **Doctorate degree**. He could now be called Dr. King. That same year, an African American named Rosa Parks was arrested. She would not give up her bus seat to a white man.

Dr. King helped Mrs. Parks. He organized a **boycott** of all the buses in Montgomery, Alabama. This made the bus companies lose money. The **law** was changed.

Some angry white people bombed Dr. King's house. Dr. King remembered Gandhi and said, "We must meet our white brother's hate with love."

Dr. King often broke **laws** that were unfair to African Americans. Many times he was put in jail. Even when he was in jail, Dr. King wrote books and letters trying to get the laws changed.

In 1963, Dr. King gave a famous speech.
He said, "I have a dream that little black
boys and black girls will be able to join
hands with little white boys and girls and
walk together as brothers and sisters."

On April 4 1968, Dr. King was shot and killed by someone who did not like the things he did. Americans everywhere **mourned** the death of this peace-loving leader.

Every year, in January, Americans celebrate Martin Luther King Jr. Day. They honor this **courageous** man who died fighting for **equal rights** for everyone.

Part Two

Dr. King worked to change **laws** that kept African Americans and whites separate. One law said that they could not drink from the same water fountain.

FOR COLORED ONLY

Martin Luther King was a popular
minister. Here he is speaking to the
members of a church.

Martin Luther King was famous after the Montgomery bus **boycott**. He gave speeches all over the United States asking for **equal rights** for everyone.

In 1964 Dr. King received the **Nobel Peace Prize** for trying peacefully to change unfair **laws**. This is a picture of him receiving it.

This is a **memorial program** from a **protest march** in Washington, D.C. in 1963. It shows when Dr. King gave his "I Have a Dream" speech.

MARCH ON WASHINGTON FOR JOBS AND FREEDOM
AUGUST 28, 1963

LINCOLN MEMORIAL PROGRAM

1.	The National Anthem	*Led by* Marian Anderson.
2.	Invocation	The Very Rev. Patrick O'Boyle, *Archbishop of Washington.*
3.	Opening Remarks	A. Philip Randolph, *Director March on Washington for Jobs and Freedom.*
4.	Remarks	Dr. Eugene Carson Blake, *Stated Clerk, United Presbyterian Church of the U.S.A.; Vice Chairman, Commission on Race Relations of the National Council of Churches of Christ in America.*
5.	Tribute to Negro Women Fighters for Freedom Daisy Bates Diane Nash Bevel Mrs. Medgar Evers Mrs. Herbert Lee Rosa Parks Gloria Richardson	Mrs. Medgar Evers
6.	Remarks	John Lewis, *National Chairman, Student Nonviolent Coordinating Committee.*
7.	Remarks	Walter Reuther, *President, United Automobile, Aerospace and Agricultural Implement Wokers of America, AFL-CIO; Chairman, Industrial Union Department, AFL-CIO.*
8.	Remarks	James Farmer, *National Director, Congress of Racial Equality.*
9.	Selection	Eva Jessye *Choir*
10.	Prayer	Rabbi Uri Miller, *President Synagogue Council of America.*
11.	Remarks	Whitney M. Young, Jr., *Executive Director, National Urban League.*
12.	Remarks	Mathew Ahmann, *Executive Director, National Catholic Conference for Interracial Justice.*
13.	Remarks	Roy Wilkins, *Executive Secretary, National Association for the Advancement of Colored People.*
14.	Selection	Miss Mahalia Jackson
15.	Remarks	Rabbi Joachim Prinz, *President American Jewish Congress.*
16.	Remarks	The Rev. Dr. Martin Luther King, Jr., *President, Southern Christian Leadership Conference.*
17.	The Pledge	A Philip Randolph
18.	Benediction	Dr. Benjamin E. Mays, *President, Morehouse College.*

"WE SHALL OVERCOME"

Dr. King wanted peaceful change, but sometimes things became violent. Here, a policeman lets his dog attack an African American during a peaceful march.

This newspaper shows when the **Civil Rights Bill** was passed. These new **laws** ended many unfair rules. It was what Martin Luther King Jr. had worked for.

The New York Times.

VOL. CXIII . No. 38,864.   © 1964 by The New York Times Company. Times Square, New York, N. Y. 10036   NEW YORK, SATURDAY, JUNE 20, 1964.   TEN CENTS

U.S. STRESSING IT WOULD FIGHT TO DEFEND ASIA

WARNING TO REDS

Commitment to Laos and South Vietnam Called Unlimited

By MAX FRANKEL
Special to The New York Times

WASHINGTON, June 19 —The Administration is saying more emphatically each day that North Vietnam and its closest ally, Communist China, must leave their neighbors alone or face a war with the United States.

In the minds of officials here the United States commitment to the security of Southeast Asia is now unlimited and comparable with the commitment to West Berlin.

In diplomatic terms this means the officials find themselves unable to negotiate with anything except the threat of force to persuade the Asian Communists to stop the efforts to "liberate" South Vietnam and Laos.

Thus far, the Administration is not sure that the Asian Communists have accurately interpreted the warning signals from Washington. It is not sure that its allies in Europe appreciate the gravity of the United States commitment. And it is not sure that the American people understand the reasons for it.

Decision Publicized

Accordingly, the word is being passed with increasing vigor to the Congress, to the Washington press corps and to the Western allies.

These official assertions suggest that the decision to deny Southeast Asia to Communism was, in effect, taken a long time ago through circumstance and a cumulative series of lesser decisions.

The view that Laos can some-

JOHNSON IS FIRM

Vows in California to Oppose Violators of Freedom in World

By TOM WICKER
Special to The New York Times

SAN FRANCISCO, June 19—President Johnson promised tonight to open an "offensive in the pursuit of peace" based on an overwhelming military power that "makes it possible to seek agreement without fearing loss of liberty."

The President, addressing an audience of nearly 2,500 at a Democratic party fund-raising dinner, also pledged stern American opposition to "those who believe they can violate their neighbor's borders and steal their neighbor's freedom."

At the end of a day in California during which he gave several indications that he expected to be President for at least four more years, Mr. Johnson said he wanted to double the size of the Peace Corps, pursue what he called the "great society" with "the vision and value of pioneers" and achieve "full equality for all our people."

Earlier in the day, after an enthusiastic welcome from more than 390,000 San Franciscans who lined Market Street to see his motorcade, the President came as near as he ever has to predicting his election in November.

Predicts the Good Life

"A Government which can get things done and knows where it is going," he said, "is the kind of Government you have had for the past four years—and that is the kind of Government you are going to get for the next four years."

Mr. Johnson's remarks were

SENATOR KENNEDY HURT IN AIR CRASH; BAYH INJURED, TOO

Both Are in Fair Condition in Massachusetts Hospital —Pilot of Plane Killed

By The Associated Press

SOUTHAMPTON, Mass., Saturday, June 20—Senator Edward M. Kennedy, younger brother of President Kennedy, and Senator Birch Bayh were injured in the crash of a private plane last night while on the way to the Massachusetts Democratic Convention.

The pilot was killed and two other persons were injured. Mr. Kennedy was semiconscious.

Both Senators were reported in fair condition at Cooley Dickinson Hospital in nearby Northampton.

Also injured were Mrs. Bayh, reported in good condition, and Edward Moss of Andover, administrative aide to Mr. Ken-

Senator Edward M. Kennedy
Associated Press

nedy, who was reported in critical condition.

The pilot was identified as Edwin J. Zimny, 48 years old, of Lawrence, a last-minute substitute for the regular Kennedy pilot.

CIVIL RIGHTS BILL PASSED, 73-27; JOHNSON URGES ALL TO COMPLY; DIRKSEN BERATES GOLDWATER

PRESIDENT'S PLEA

He Declares the Task Now Is to Change Law Into Custom

Special to The New York Times

SAN FRANCISCO, June 19—President Johnson called the Senate passage of his civil rights bill today a "challenge to men of good will in every part of the country to transform the commands of our law into the customs of our land."

Mr. Johnson said it was now the nation's task "to reach beyond the content of the bill to conquer the barriers of poor education, poverty, and squalid housing which are an inheritance of past injustice and an impediment to future advance."

He said that he did not underestimate the depth of the passions involved in the struggle for racial equality."

But he also spoke of "a large reservoir of goodwill and compassion, of decency and fair play which seeks a vision of justice without violence in the streets."

Johnson Statement

If these forces, the President said, "do not desert the field, if they can be brought to the battle, then the years of trial will be a prelude to the final triumph of a land with liberty and justice for all."

The President issued his statement on the rights bill here, while he was beginning a two-day tour of California. The full text of the statement follows:

"Senate passage of the civil rights bill is a major step toward equal opportunities for all Americans. I congratulate Senators of both parties who worked to make passage pos-

ON HAND FOR THE VOTE: Visitors waiting outside the Capitol yesterday for admittance to the Senate Chamber, before the vote on the civil rights bill was registered.
United Press International Telephoto

ARIZONAN TARGET OF GOP LEADER   Rights Bill Roll-Call Vote
By The Associated Press

ACTION BY SENATE

Revised Measure Now Goes Back to House for Concurrence

By E. W. KENWORTHY
Special to The New York Times

WASHINGTON, June 19 —The Senate passed the civil rights bill today by a vote of 73 to 27.

The final roll-call came at 7:40 P.M. on the 83d day of debate, nine days after closure was invoked.

Voting for the bill were 46 Democrats and 27 Republicans. Voting against it were 21 Democrats and six Republicans. Except for Senator Robert C. Byrd of West Virginia, all the Democratic votes against the bill came from Southerners.

Senator Barry Goldwater of Arizona voted against the bill, as he said yesterday he would. The five other Republicans opposing it all support Mr. Goldwater's candidacy for the Republican Presidential nomination.

They were Bourke B. Hickenlooper of Iowa, chairman of the Senate Republican Policy Committee; Norris Cotton of New Hampshire, Edwin L. Mechem of New Mexico, Milward L. Simpson of Wyoming and John G. Tower of Texas.

2 Pledge Acceptance

The bill will now go back to the House for concurrence in the changes that the Senate made in the measure the House passed last Feb. 10 by a vote of 290 to 130.

Tonight, Representatives Emanuel Celler, Democrat of New York, and William M. McCulloch, Republican of Ohio, who are the chairman and

Every day hundreds of people visit
Dr. King's gravesite. The words cut into
the stone say, "Free at Last, Free at Last.
Thank God Almighty, I am Free at Last."

Glossary

This glossary explains difficult words, and helps you to say words which may be hard to say.

boycott Stop going to a store or using a service to protest.

civil rights bill Law which makes sure people are treated fairly.

courageous Brave. You say *kur ay jus*.

doctorate degree Highest college degree a person can receive.

equal rights Everyone having the same rights, no matter what their race or religion is.

laws Rules.

march Group of people walking together to show their support for something.

memorial programs List of what happens at a special event. You say *meh mor ee uhl*.

minister Priest.

mourned Feel sad when someone dies.

Nobel Peace Prize Award given each year to a person who works for peace.

nonviolent Not being violent or fighting back.

protest Complain about an unfair law.

seminary College for people studying to become religious leaders. You say *SEM uh nair ee*.

Index

More Books to Read

Adler, David. *A Picture Book of Martin Luther King, Jr.* New York: Holiday, 1989.

Bray, Rosemary L. *Martin Luther King.* New York: Greenwillow, 1995.

Greene, Carol. *Martin Luther King, Jr. A Man Who Changed Things.* Chicago: Childrens Press, 1989.